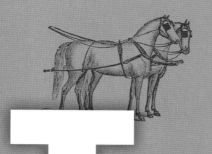

THE HISTORY OF
TRANSPORTATION

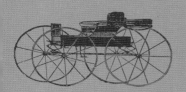

Judith Herbst

TWENTY-FIRST CENTURY BOOKS

Minneapolis

Twenty-First Century Books
A division of Lerner Publishing Group
241 First Avenue North
Minneapolis, MN 55401 U.S.A.

Website address: www.lernerbooks.com

Library of Congress Cataloging-in-Publication Data

Herbst, Judith.
      The history of transportation / by Judith Herbst.
          p.   cm. — (Major inventions through history)
      Includes bibliographical references and index.
      ISBN-13: 978–0–8225–2496–0 (lib. bdg. : alk. paper)
      ISBN-10: 0–8225–2496–1 (lib. bdg. : alk. paper)
      1. Transportation—History. 2. Vehicles—History. I. Title. II. Series.
   HE151.H445 2006
   388'.09—dc22   2004023020

Manufactured in the United States of America
1 2 3 4 5 6 – DP – 11 10 09 08 07 06

CONTENTS

Introduction

In our quest for food, riches, knowledge, and adventure, we have traveled many billions of miles. We covered some miles on foot, chasing animals for our dinner. But our curiosity led us to imagine wonderful ways to travel farther. We built boats to cross wide rivers and vast oceans. We designed wheeled vehicles powered by steam, electricity, and gasoline. We invented airplanes so we could fly through the air like birds. We figured out how to travel under the sea and even up to the moon.

Transportation inventions have changed the face of the land, and they have changed us. Every day we are being transported into the future. Listen. You can hear the rumble of the wheels.

CHAPTER 1

The Wheel

Whoever invented the wheel could never have known what a big hit it was going to be. No invention has had a greater impact on civilization. Take it away, and so much else disappears with it. You'd still be able to get around, of course. You could walk or ride your ox. But forget about your scooter, skateboard, and in-line skates. They all have wheels. You couldn't hop on a plane, take the bus, or hail a

taxi. You couldn't even climb into a wheelbarrow and ask someone to push you. In fact, life would be so simple, you might just as well be in Mesopotamia, oh, say, about 5,500 years ago. . . .

A Slow Start

Mesopotamia was an ancient region of the Middle East, covering modern-day Iraq and eastern Syria. Mesopotamia grew to be a great civilization, but in 3500 B.C., things were still a little slow. The people farmed and made pots out of clay. In fact, someone had just invented a round turntable for shaping the clay. He or she had no idea that this simple wooden wheel was about to go places.

Time passed. Making pottery had gotten much easier, but hauling things was still hard. The Mesopotamians were pulling wooden sledges (large, sturdy sleds) fitted with runners to move stones and other heavy objects. But when the sledge was full, it took every ounce of strength just to get it moving. From time to time, people must have wondered if these sledges could be improved. But it took a while before some clever person removed the runners and replaced them with wheels.

The world's oldest-known wheel is from 3500 B.C. in Mesopotamia.

Humans domesticate
the horse.

ca. 4000 B.C.

The wheel is invented in
Mesopotamia.

3500 B.C.

WHOA!

The horse was one of the last species of livestock to be domesticated, or taught to live with humans. The horse was probably first hunted for food. Then, probably by 4000 B.C., it was kept by herders in many places as a source of meat and milk. By about 3000 B.C., horses had begun to pull plows and then, finally, people.

The idea was so brilliant, you'd think that everybody would have quickly hitched their oxen to these wheeled carts and started going places. But carts, like sledges, were not yet thought of as vehicles for people. They were only used to transport goods or heavy objects a short distance. People walked or traveled on the backs of oxen. Because there weren't any roads yet, why bother with a cart? It would only get stuck in the mud.

There's another reason why wheeled carts didn't immediately catch on as a means of transportation. The cities in Mesopotamia and Egypt were built next to great rivers. The Tigris and the Euphrates rivers cut through Mesopotamia, and the Nile River runs the entire length of Egypt. Sailing down a swift river made more sense than trying to keep a cart moving slowly over uneven ground.

The wheel didn't change people's lives too much until about 3000 B.C. That's when the Mesopotamians invented the chariot, a two-wheeled cart pulled by a horse. At first, chariots were used in royal funeral processions. But it soon occurred to army commanders that chariots would be a great way to surprise the enemy.

Mesopotamians invent the chariot.

3000 B.C.

Armies could roll in, attack, and then thunder off into the sunset.

The use of chariots spread quickly to China and Europe. In Greece and Rome, chariot racing became very popular. Centuries later, it became the main event in the Greek Olympic Games and the Roman circus games.

Laying Down Tracks

In 312 B.C., the Romans began building what would become 50,000 miles (80,500 kilometers) of stone roads. The first of these roads was the Via Appia (the Appian Way). It ran 162 miles (261 km) from Rome to the eastern city of Taranto (then called Tarentum). Over the centuries, the Roman Empire brought more and more territories under its control. The road system extended out from Rome to modern-day Great Britain, Romania, Greece, Iraq, and North Africa. It was, indeed, true that "all roads led to Rome."

The Roman roads encouraged trade between distant cities and put people in touch with each other. Travel to and from Rome along the straight, well-drained roads was easy and direct. By law, everyone was free to use the roads, but the people in each Roman

ADDING SPOKES

The first wheels were made from three solid pieces of wood fitted together in the shape of a circle. They were almost too heavy to be useful. Then people discovered a way to make them lighter. They cut out most of the wood from inside the circle and replaced it with wooden bars called spokes. Vehicles with spoked wheels were faster and easier to manage.

The Romans begin building the Via Appia, one of the world's first road systems.
312 B.C.

province had to maintain them. Most did a fairly good job—at least for a while. By the Middle Ages (about A.D. 500 to 1500), the roads had begun to crumble, but they still served the empire well. Fragments of the great Roman roads survive to this day.

The longest road in the ancient world wasn't actually just one road. It was a trade route—several roads, usually close together, used for trading goods between regions. Much of the route opened for travelers in the second century B.C. The route started in eastern China and ran through Tibet and Persia (modern-day Iran), all the way to Rome (in modern-day Italy). Ox-drawn and horse-drawn vehicles traveled in groups called caravans, back and forth along the 4000-mile (6,400 km) route. The vehicles were laden with wool, gold, and silver. But it was silk from China that gave this magnificent trade route its name: the Silk Road. Ideas also traveled along the Silk Road. It was a great way for people from

Chinese traders use a magnetic compass to find their way.

A.D. 1090

different countries to share literature, scientific discoveries, and inventions with each other.

Stagecoaches

For centuries the wheeled cart was fairly simple and functional. Then, in the 1500s, the first four-wheeled coaches were built in Hungary, in Eastern Europe. Unlike a hard, often rickety, work cart, the Hungarian coach was comfortable and elegant. Its wood was polished and gleaming, not rough and full of slivers. Riders sat on cushioned seats while strong, sturdy horses pulled the coach along. "Wow!" said the wealthy British upper class. "That's for us!" They began ordering the Hungarian coaches in huge numbers. Then British craftsmen learned to build their own fine coaches. Before long, the new industry was going strong in both places.

The less wealthy also liked the idea of riding in a fancy coach, but they couldn't afford to buy one. And few people had the means to feed and take care of more than one horse. But this gave some clever business owners the idea of a coach-for-hire service. They opened livery stables, where customers could rent horses and carriages. These coaches-for-hire were the model for modern taxicabs.

By the 1600s, coaches were traveling along fixed routes in England, making regular stops at stations along the way. These stations were called stages, and so the coaches became stagecoaches. Until stagecoaches came along, traveling either on foot or by horseback wasn't

The first four-wheeled coaches are built in Hungary.
1500s

Stagecoaches travel along fixed routes in England.
1600s

STAND AND DELIVER!

In seventeenth-century England, highway robbery was common. In fact, coach travelers could pretty much count on being held up by pistol-waving highwaymen. Highwaymen would force coaches to stop along the road. Then, with a shout of "stand and deliver," they'd demand that passengers get out of the coach and hand over all their money and jewelry. How did these "land pirates" get away with their crimes? Rural England had long stretches of deserted road. At night they were deserted, *unlit* roads. And rural law enforcement usually consisted of ordinary citizens who took turns keeping the peace. Highwaymen were faster, better armed, and more willing to take risks than either their victims or law officers.

much fun. Getting anywhere took a long time, and travelers were rained and snowed on. But in a stagecoach, passengers could relax and watch the scenery while they covered more territory than ever before in a shorter amount of time.

A few inns (what we'd call hotels) already existed. But as more stagecoach routes were added, the number of inns increased in towns along the routes. Local merchants were also glad to welcome a steady stream of new customers. Some began carrying more and different items to sell, and some even enlarged their stores. Little businesses grew into bigger businesses.

Mail Call

Coaches helped businesses in another way too. Britain began moving from a farming culture to a manufacturing society in the eighteenth century. A quick, reliable way to send and receive

New inventions and technology begin to change Britain into a manufacturing society.

1760s

business letters became very important. But before coaches, sending a letter to someone was hit or miss.

In Britain postriders carried mail from town to town on horseback or on foot. The mail moved very slowly and didn't always reach its destination. But things really changed with the British Post Office Act of 1765. This new law made it a crime to carry the mail slower than 6 miles (10 km) an hour. So stagecoaches took over the job. And businesses weren't the only ones that benefited. More reliable mail also helped family and friends keep in touch.

The Phoenix Line "safety coach" travels between Washington, D.C., and Baltimore, Maryland, in the mid-1800s.

Stagecoaches take over mail delivery after a British post office act.

1765

In early America, the mail also went by stagecoach. But as soon as outlaws learned that stagecoaches often carried money and other valuables, they started robbing them. Stagecoach drivers took to carrying rifles, which made for a rather exciting trip. But people kept riding coaches anyway. They liked the idea that they could travel so far from home and actually sit on a real seat.

Headed West

By the mid-1800s, the United States was pushing west into the territories that became California, Oregon, and Washington. In 1848 the discovery of gold at Sutter's Mill in California acted like a powerful magnet, drawing fortune seekers west. Other people were simply curious about what might lie beyond the Rocky Mountains. Still others wanted to build farms or ranches on the vast lands of the western territories.

These adventurous pioneers traveled in large canvas-covered wagons pulled by oxen or horses. Everything they owned was inside, along with grandma, grandpa, and all the kids. For the

THE COVERED WAGON

The Conestoga wagon (often called the covered wagon) was also used to haul cargo in the early eighteenth century. It was designed and built in a part of Pennsylvania that was home to the Conestoga Indians. In its time, the Conestoga wagon was a monster vehicle. When one was fully loaded, it took six horses to pull it.

Pioneers head west to the
U.S. Pacific coast.
1840s

Pioneers cross the Great Plains of the United States in covered wagons in the mid-1800s.

first time in U.S. history, entire families relocated to another part of the country. The pioneers brought with them their skills, talents, and customs. They staked claims and developed the land. Towns sprang up, with banks, stores, hotels, and other businesses.

And this great movement didn't only happen in the United States. The wheel had changed the face of nearly every country on the globe. By helping people go places, it put them in touch with each other. And there was no turning back.

What would the wheel's inventor have thought if he or she could have watched the movement of so many people on this simple invention? "Wow! Look what I made!" probably sums it up.

CHAPTER 2

The Sail

Even the earliest humans knew that things floated. Water lilies and nutshells, for example. And logs. Especially logs. Animals might sit on them. Big waves could wash over them. But they always stayed on top of the water, happily sailing along with the current. This, our ancestors realized, was a great way to travel.

The first boats were hollowed-out tree trunks and were probably used for fishing. A hungry person with a spear and a sharp eye could

wade only so far into the water. But a boat, he discovered, enlarged his fishing range and kept him dry at the same time. If he used paddles, he could go even farther. And, of course, a boat gave him a place to put all his fish.

By 3500 B.C., the very first cities of Mesopotamia had begun to spring up along the Tigris and Euphrates rivers. (Mesopotamia means "between two rivers.") The Tigris and Euphrates run all the way from Turkey to the Persian Gulf, a distance of more than 1,000 miles (1,610 km).

Many early boats were dugouts, or hollowed-out logs from large trees. This is an image of an early Native American canoe in the Pacific Northwest.

Cities spring up along the
Tigris and Euphrates rivers.
3500 B.C.

RAFTING DOWN THE NILE

Rafts are even older than dugout boats. They were trickier to steer, but they had a lot more room. The ancient Egyptians probably used rafts to transport enormous blocks of stone from quarries to pyramid construction sites.

The Mesopotamians, as you know, had just invented the wheel, but they weren't using it for transportation. They didn't need it. They were already traveling great distances in small, reliable boats made from reeds, the dried stems of certain plants. At first, men pulling oars powered the boats. Then people realized that a good stiff wind could do the same job. But how could they capture that wind?

The sail was invented sometime around 3000 B.C. But the first sails weren't made of cloth. Mesopotamians and Egyptians used the most common local material—papyrus, a plant that grows throughout the Nile and Tigris and Euphrates river valleys. Even though the sails were simple papyrus reed mats stretched between two poles, they worked quite well. The Mesopotamians and Egyptians quickly learned to harness the wind and navigate their rivers. This allowed them to trade with cities they couldn't reach on foot.

With sails instead of muscles doing the work, boats could be a lot bigger. The Phoenicians, who lived along the Mediterranean Sea coast in modern-day Lebanon, became the great sailors of the ancient world. By 1200 B.C., the Phoenicians were building 80-foot-long (24-meter) wooden cargo vessels with enormous cloth sails. A ship this size

The papyrus reed sail is invented.

3000 B.C.

Phoenicians sail around the tip of Africa.

600 B.C.

could carry a fairly large crew great distances. The Phoenicians made their way out into the Atlantic and as far north as Great Britain and Ireland. By 600 B.C., they had gone completely around Africa. Once human beings learned to sail, they were determined to explore.

The Age of Exploration

The great Age of Exploration began with Christopher Columbus in A.D. 1492. Columbus was looking for a trade route to Asia. But he wound up sailing to the Bahamas, islands off the coast of modern-day Florida. That was okay, though. Columbus liked the region and returned three more times.

English, Italian, and Portuguese explorers followed Columbus west. By the early 1500s, maps were being completely redrawn to include such places as Labrador, Newfoundland, the Delaware Bay, and the Yucatan Peninsula in Mexico. Europeans had not even known these places existed. The world was turning out to look much different than most people thought.

Unfortunately, European sailors brought more than their lunch to the lands they had discovered. They also brought diseases, such

VIKING VOYAGES

Between the ninth and eleventh centuries A.D., the Vikings built some of the biggest and best ships. The Vikings were Danes, Swedes, and Norwegians. Their idea of adventure was to sail to the British Isles, France, and Germany and stage bloodthirsty raids. Thanks to their seaworthy ships, they were also able to reach and establish settlements in Iceland, Greenland, and North America.

Vikings explore the North Atlantic Ocean in ships.

A.D. 900

An expedition led by Christopher Columbus comes upon the Bahamas.

1492

as smallpox, that spread from person to person. Native Americans had no natural resistance—the way a human body fights off a disease—to smallpox. The disease ran through the native populations like a wildfire, killing huge numbers of people.

DEAD RECKONING

The earliest sailors navigated, or found their way, by the stars. But that only worked at night when it wasn't cloudy. Mostly, sailors used dead reckoning, and it was far from accurate. A ship's current position was calculated from its previous position. So, every change of speed and course had to be written down and plotted. Sailors made a lot of mistakes, which is why they often lost places they thought they had discovered.

Another terrible side effect of sea exploration was the rapid growth of slavery. European countries founded colonies in these newly discovered regions in the Americas, which were often rich in natural resources. The colonists mined for gold and diamonds, and they planted huge farms of sugar, coffee, and cotton. The colonists needed cheap labor for these mines and plantations. They began using African men, women, and children who had been captured in Africa, transported on ships to the Americas, and forced into slavery there. The African slave trade was widespread and involved millions of slaves.

But sails also brought settlers looking for a better life across the ocean. In 1607 the London Company hired Captain Christopher Newport to bring settlers to North America. By 1700 one-quarter

Settlers from Europe establish colonies in North America.

1600s

of a million people had moved from England and established new colonies. The French had settled in Mississippi and Louisiana. And William Penn had purchased a big chunk of Pennsylvania from the Delaware Indians.

If it hadn't been for the sail, none of these people would have made it to North America. The journey was simply too far, and the ocean was impossible to cross in a boat powered only by oars. The sail allowed vastly different cultures to mix, sometimes with good results, sometimes with bad.

People also learned that if they had the right stuff, there was no place on earth they couldn't go, including the North Pole. The wheel may have opened up countries, but it was the sail that opened up the world.

CHAPTER 3

The Steam Engine

A fierce gang of troublemakers sailed the trade routes in the 1300s. Rats. They hid in the lower levels of ships among the barrels of spices and food and bundles of silks. They overran the ships and streamed onto the docks. Rats carried fleas in their hides, and the fleas carried a disease called the plague.

Throughout history, the plague has been one of the most horrifying diseases to strike humans. It is caused by bacteria that infect the fleas that live on rats. Infected fleas jump from rats to humans.

When a flea bites a human, it deposits countless plague bacteria into the person's bloodstream. In a few days, the symptoms show up: shivering, vomiting, headache, high fever, and swelling in the groin, neck, and armpits. Sometimes the patient recovers. But often not, and death is often painful.

From 1347 to 1351, the Black Death, as the plague was called, roared through Europe. By the time it was over, one-third of the population had died, leaving Europe with a serious labor shortage. With fewer people to do the work, there was suddenly an urgent need to find new ways to get jobs done. The cleverest minds in Europe got busy.

Over the next three centuries, European inventors worked on designing engines. An engine is a machine that converts energy into mechanical motion. A windmill, for example, uses wind to spin its blades or sails. That motion, in turn, is used as power to pump water or grind grain. By creating power, engines help or even replace human and animal workers. But inventors wanted to build an engine that created its own energy and didn't rely on an outside source such as wind. And they turned their minds to an energy source familiar to anyone who's ever boiled a pot of water.

Steamboat's A-Comin'!

In 1690 French scientist Denis Papin figured out how to harness the energy of steam. He built a very simple steam engine called a digester. James Watt, a Scottish inventor, developed this engine to

The Black Death begins to
spread across Europe.

1347

Denis Papin develops a
simple steam engine.

1690

make it more practical. In 1769 he filed a patent (a claim to legal rights for an invention) for the first modern steam engine. Soon after, engineers and inventors began producing designs for steam-driven boats. The machine age was about to dawn.

In 1786 John Fitch built and tested the first American steamboat. Four years later, he was running a regular passenger and freight service on the Delaware River in New York and New Jersey. Unfortunately, Fitch didn't pay much attention to the costs of

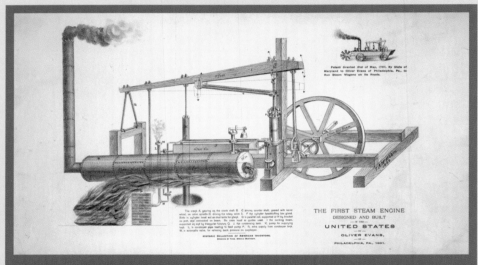

This drawing shows the first steam engine built in the United States. It was designed by Oliver Evans, an American inventor and millwright, in 1801. Evans's engine differed from James Watt's engine in that it used high pressure rather than low pressure.

James Watt patents the first
modern steam engine.

1769

John Fitch builds the first
American steamboat.

1786

building and running his boats, and he soon went out of business.

Robert Fulton picked up where Fitch left off. In 1807 Fulton's boat the *Clermont* made a five-hour trip up the Hudson River from New York City to Albany, New York. By 1814 Fulton's steamboats were traveling up and down the lower Mississippi River. Fulton's boats were paddle wheel steamboats. Steam was produced in the belly of the boat by heating water in a large boiler over a coal fire. The steam in turn drove a large wooden wheel fitted with paddles at the back of the boat. The paddle wheel pushed the boat forward in the water. Paddle wheel steamboats became the most efficient way to move goods and people up and down the Mississippi.

As boilers improved, so did steamboats. Steamboats became common on canals and rivers in the United States and throughout the British Isles. Heavy cargo was moving faster and farther than ever before.

The British government was quick to see the commercial value of larger steamships that could travel across oceans. In 1836 the newly formed Great Western Steamship Company began construction on

> ### QUICK QUIZ
> The first steamboat sailed down which body of water? If you guessed the Mississippi River, ooh la la, you are wrong. It was the Seine River in France. Marquis Claude Francois de Jouffroy d'Abbans demonstrated his paddle wheel steamboat on the Seine in 1783.

Robert Fulton sails the *Clermont* up the Hudson River.

1807

Construction begins on the *Great Western*, the first oceangoing steamship.

1836

the first oceangoing steamship. Two years later, the *Great Western* left Bristol, England. It arrived in New York City fifteen days later. On a sailing ship, the transatlantic voyage would have taken more than one month.

The British government quickly backed the establishment of four steamship lines. Each would cover a different shipping lane and keep to a regular schedule. By 1840 British steamships were crisscrossing the world's oceans, carrying cargo to and from every continent except Antarctica.

Britain's shipbuilding industry boomed. Thousands found work in the shipyards as ironworkers and carpenters. Many more lined up to be hired as workers on board the ships once they sailed. Dockworkers were also needed to load and unload the ships in port. And those who invested in these newfangled steamships found themselves getting very rich very quickly.

Once the steam engine replaced the heavy sails and tall masts,

TRANSATLANTIC CABLES

Steamships created a new era in the history of travel between Europe and North America. But a steamship also made history in the field of communications. In 1866 the *Great Eastern* was loaded with 2,700 miles (4,345 km) of specially coated telegraph cable weighing 5,000 tons (4,536 metric tons). On its journey across the Atlantic, the *Great Eastern* laid the cable on the ocean floor from Ireland to Newfoundland, Canada. Telegraph offices used the transatlantic cable to send telegrams across the ocean. Telegrams took a few hours to transmit, but that was still a lot faster than sending a letter.

British steamships sail to every continent except Antarctica.
1840

A group of Norwegian immigrants waits aboard S.S. *Angelo*, a steamship bound for the United States.

ships could be bigger than ever before. The steamers that sailed from Britain in the nineteenth century were 2,000-ton (1,800-metric-ton) giants. The ships had three or four decks and could accommodate large numbers of passengers. Thousands of European immigrants began using these ships to cross the Atlantic Ocean, changing the face of North America forever.

The Little Engine That Could—and Did

Around the same time inventors began using steam to drive boats, other inventors were working on using the same technology on land.

The first few steam locomotives were clumsy and slow, but they were perfect for England's coal mines. Up to this point, mined coal had been hauled out of the pits in wheeled carts pulled by horses. But George Stephenson, a miner in England, realized that a locomotive could do a better job than a team of horses. In 1814 Stephenson built a locomotive that could pull 30 tons (27 metric tons) uphill at 4 miles (6.4 km) an hour.

The locomotive revolutionized the British coal industry. It not only pulled the loads of coal out of the mines, but it could be used to ship coal across Britain. By train, coal could be sent directly to cities. By the early nineteenth century, cities were gobbling up coal like hungry monsters to heat homes and feed the boilers in the growing number of factories.

When the Liverpool & Manchester Railway officially opened on September 15, 1830, the directors were delightfully shocked. The railway had planned to haul freight over the 31 miles

TIME TO GO!

In the 1800s, when trains started running on regular schedules, a standardized system of timekeeping had to be established. Before then, time had been a rather loose affair. Most people set their routines according to morning, afternoon, or evening. Nobody really needed to be anywhere or do anything on the dot. But when train travel became popular, the dots counted. Trains arrived and departed at exact times. Accurate watches, synchronized (set to the same time) clocks, timetables, and schedules became important for the first time.

Britain's Great Western Railway carries ten thousand passengers per week.

1840s

(50 km) that separated the British cities of Liverpool and Manchester. But an excited public clamored for a ride. Railroads were about to provide transportation service for their first passengers.

In comparison, horse-drawn coaches and wagons were downright poky. On very long trips, several stops had to be made to change horses. That slowed things down even more. Wagons and coaches were dusty and bumpy. But train travel was fast and comfortable. On average, it cut travel time in half. And for just 10 shillings (about $1.20), you could buy a first-class ticket. No wonder the cry, "All aboard!" was so attractive, not only in Britain, but in other parts of Europe and the United States too.

For merchants and manufacturers, locomotives were a dream come true. A locomotive could haul several times the amount of freight carried in a horse-drawn wagon. As steam engines improved, more train cars were added. Even better, different kinds of freight could be shipped together. Cattle could travel with sacks of feed without the danger of the feed being eaten. Just put them in different cars.

Locomotives also pulled a new kind of train car called a refrigerator car. The refrigerator car carried huge blocks of ice, which kept the whole car cold. The cars were built to carry meat and other perishables long distances. For the first time, food could travel across the country and reach its destination chilled and fresh.

The railroads also brought great economic growth. People invested in the railroads and made huge amounts of money.

Dozens of new types of jobs became available. Workers were needed to lay track. Engineers were needed to drive the trains. Firemen shoveled the coal into the boilers. Conductors collected passenger tickets and announced station stops. And people found work in the railroad yards, making sure train traffic ran smoothly and safely.

Even the landscape changed. Railway tunnels were blasted out of rock so cities could be put on line. Train bridges were built over rivers to carry the thundering locomotives. One of the greatest achievements of the 1800s was the completion of the transcontinental railroad in the United States. It connected the East Coast to the West Coast and carried more people across the country than a hundred wagon trains. All along the line, towns sprang up like mushrooms.

Nothing did more than the locomotive to fill out countries such as the United States. The 1800s were truly golden, crackling with excitement, enthusiasm, and growth. Could things possibly get any better?

Oh boy. Just wait.

The First Transcontinental Railroad across the United States is completed.

1869

CHAPTER 4
The Internal Combustion Engine

By 1818 the wheel had been around for more than five thousand years. Baron Karl Drais von Sauerbronn of Germany gave it a new spin.

Von Sauerbronn's idea was to attach two wheels to a bar and place a little seat about midway between them. The wheels were the same size, but the front wheel was steerable. Von Sauerbronn called his funny-looking vehicle a Draisine, named after himself, naturally. After a while, it came to be known as a hobbyhorse or a dandy horse. The public immediately fell in love with it.

Bicycles have come a long way since the late 1800s, when many had larger front wheels than rear wheels.

Over the years, dozens of people improved on von Sauerbronn's basic design. Pedals were added, and brakes and air-filled tires came along. The front wheel got very large, and the rear wheel shrank. Finally, the wheels ended up being the same size again, and gears were attached. The vehicle had many names, but the one that stuck was bicycle.

The bicycle led to the development of the motorcycle, which first ran on steam. The L. D. Copeland Company of Philadelphia,

High-wheel bicycles become a popular fad with young men worldwide.

1880s

Pennsylvania, cranked out about two hundred of these "steam tricycles." But in the second half of the nineteenth century, inventors began working on another power source for vehicles—the internal combustion engine.

Rather than heating water to produce steam, an internal combustion engine burns a high-energy fuel called gasoline. When mixed with air and ignited, gasoline produces a quick and powerful explosion. Throughout the 1860s and 1870s, inventors worked on ways to turn these explosions into mechanical energy that could power machines and vehicles.

In 1885 Gottlieb Daimler and Wilhelm Maybach of Germany attached an internal combustion engine to a wooden bicycle frame. They had created the first gasoline-driven motorcycle. Over the next two years, Daimler and Maybach worked on speeding up the engine's combustion process—the release of energy from the ignited gasoline. More rapid energy bursts meant more power. In 1887 Daimler and Maybach filed a patent for their high-speed engine.

The Automobile

The high-speed internal combustion engine was a leap forward for the automobile. Automobiles, or motorcars, had been around for a while. Early models ran on steam or batteries, and they looked like a sleigh with wheels. The new gasoline-powered motorcars didn't

Daimler and Maybach
design the first gas-driven
motorcycle.

1885

immediately replace these earlier models. For a few decades, they shared the roads.

For example, the Stanley Steamer (built by the Stanley brothers of Maine) was the talk of the town and actually moved at a pretty good clip. It even set a record at the Daytona, Florida, racecourse for the fastest mile—28.2 seconds (1.6 km in 28.2 seconds). That's 127 miles (204 km) per hour. But eventually, gasoline proved a better fuel than steam. Gas-powered autos could go faster and farther than steam-driven models.

In Europe companies such as Daimler, Benz, Peugeot, Renault, and Fiat spent the 1890s designing their own models and working on engine improvements. In the United States, some of the first gas-powered autos were built in the mid-1890s by Charles and Frank Duryea, bicycle makers from Massachusetts. A Michigan engineer named Henry Ford also got in on the act. He built his first "horseless carriage" in 1896.

CAR-SPEAK

The automobile has changed the way we speak. Here's a sampling. A *spare tire* is that extra bit of flab around your waist. A *sparkplug* is an energetic person who makes things happen, and a *backseat driver* is someone who gives advice without being asked. *Step on it* means "hurry up!" and if you're *running on empty,* you're exhausted. When you're *in the driver's seat*, you're in control, and when you *shift gears,* you change what you're doing. A *fender bender* is a minor accident, and *rubbernecking* is slowing down to stare at an accident.

Henry Ford builds his first
horseless carriage.
1896

By the time Ford opened his motor company in Michigan in 1903, quite a few cars were already in use. But each had been made to order and hand-built. Production took a long time and was very expensive, so only wealthy people had cars. Ford realized that automobiles would never be affordable for the average person unless they were produced faster and in great numbers.

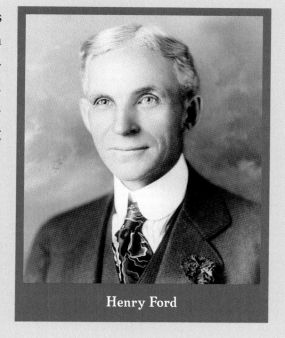
Henry Ford

In 1913 Ford began using an assembly line to build cars in his factory. On an assembly line, ropes pulled a car frame past workers stationed along the line. Each worker added a part or did a particular job. The time it took to assemble a car was cut in half, from twelve and one-half hours to just six.

Ford also cut costs and time by offering few or no special options. Almost all his Model Ts were exactly alike. In fact, the car only came in one color—black. By mass-producing this basic model, Ford made it possible for more people to afford an automobile. And it worked. Ford sold millions of Model Ts.

Ford begins selling
Model T automobiles.

1908

Ford installs assembly lines
in his Michigan auto factory.

1913

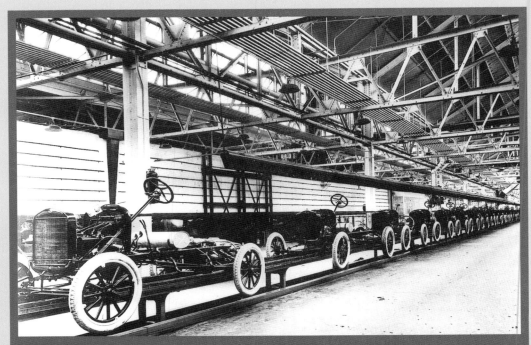

Partially built cars await finishing touches on the Ford Motor Company's assembly line in the early 1900s.

The number of car sales soon led to drivers' biggest headache: traffic. Fortunately, Garrett Morgan of Ohio had a solution. Morgan came up with the idea for a three-way automatic traffic light. This controlled the flow of motor cars as well as the thousands of bicycles that were still on the road. People trying to cross streets on foot were also grateful. They had been dashing out of

Garrett Morgan patents his
traffic signal.
1923

the way of self-taught drivers. It would take a while before people would be legally required to earn drivers' licenses.

The early cars had neither a roof nor a windshield, so driving was messy. The roads were basically dirt, and when it rained, they turned to mud. Loose stones flew up and hit the passengers. Ruts and bumps jostled them. It was painfully clear that cities and towns had to start laying down some decent roads.

Road Maps, Road Hogs, Road Rage, and Roads

As the number of automobile owners grew, so did the number of highways. Bridges and tunnels were constructed across the United States so motorists didn't have to stop for rivers, high mountains, or deep canyons. When roads began to crisscross each other, highway engineers built overpasses—roads on two levels so traffic wouldn't have to stop at intersections.

Cars were becoming faster, bigger, and more comfortable, and people wanted to go places. All this traveling gave us road maps, rest stops, motels (motor hotels), mobile homes and trailer parks, drive-up windows, toll booths, speed limits, car insurance, parking meters, parking tickets, and traffic court.

Carts, wagons, and carriages served as the first trucks, but the internal combustion engine turned trucking into an industry. Even though trucks couldn't haul as much cargo as a string of railroad cars, trucks had the freedom to go wherever the highways

The Airstream Company
introduces its Clipper
vacation trailer.
1936

THE INTERSTATE

The United States is crisscrossed by a network of highways known as the interstate system. There are 43,000 miles (69,200 km) of interstate highway, making it the largest engineered structure in history. Drivers can travel from Maine to Florida on I-95 (that is, Interstate 95), passing through sixteen states on the way. I-90 runs more than 3,000 miles (4,830 km), from Boston, Massachusetts, to Seattle, Washington. With high speed limits and special entrances and exits, the interstate system provides fast, direct car travel. But in some large cities, the interstates are so crowded during rush hours that traffic moves slower than a horse-drawn carriage would.

took them. Trucks could pick up freight from railroad yards and distribute it to warehouses, stores, and local businesses. Trucks also began carrying the mail. These days, trucks transport just about anything you can think of—from chickens to chemicals.

With thousands and then hundreds of thousands of gasoline-driven vehicles on the road, an oil industry arose to meet the growing need for fuel. Filling stations started popping up. Everything related to building or servicing cars grew.

It's impossible to list all the ways the internal combustion engine has changed our lives. But you can get a feel for it the next time you're in a car riding through town. Imagine that the internal combustion engine has never been invented. What

U.S. president Dwight D. Eisenhower signs the Interstate Highway Act.
1956

A filling station crew poses in tiny Creal Springs, Illinois, in 1942. As more roads were built across the United States, stations popped up even in small country towns.

would disappear? Here are a few examples to start you off. The stop sign at the end of the block, the parking lot at the mall, garages, the drive-up window at McDonald's, the car wash, tractors, lawn mowers, snowblowers, and of course, the very car in which you are riding.

McDonald's opens its first drive-up window in Sierra Vista, Arizona.
1975

CHAPTER 5

The Airplane

The internal combustion engine was not yet finished changing the world. It had one more mission.

When the twentieth century began, Orville and Wilbur Wright had a nice little business in North Carolina building bicycles. But bicycles rode along the ground. Orville and Wilbur wanted to soar above the trees. So they had a chat with Charles Taylor, who worked in their bicycle shop. Could he help them build a little engine? Yes, he said, he certainly could.

The Wright brothers took off on December 17, 1903, in a 600-pound (272-kilogram) wood, wire, and cloth airplane. Taylor's four-cylinder, twelve-horsepower engine was strapped on to the plane's body. The engine might have been small, but it was enough to get the plane off the ground. The trip lasted twelve seconds.

The Wright brothers covered about 120 feet (37 m) on their first try. By 2004 an Airbus A340-500 passenger jet could cross almost 10,000 miles (16,100 km) without refueling. Airplanes carry us farther and faster than any other form of transportation (except for the space shuttle). Every day in the United States, 14,600 planes take off, not counting military flights and private aircraft. The air is filled with the roar of jet engines. But it all started very quietly in a city park in Paris, France.

Lighter than Air

On a crisp autumn day in 1783, a gigantic hot-air balloon rose above the colorful trees in the Bois de Boulogne, a large park on the western edge of Paris. A basket hung beneath the balloon, carrying a scientist, Jean-Francois Pilatre de Rozier, and a nobleman, the Marquis d'Arlandes. The Montgolfier brothers had designed the balloon and were on hand for the launch. But they were apparently too scared to ride in their airship. They probably regretted it. The scientist and the nobleman had a great adventure and returned to earth safely. It was the first time human beings had actually flown.

The Montgolfier brothers
launch their hot-air balloon
in Paris, France.

1783

As a means of transportation, however, hot-air balloons never got off the ground. They were just not practical. Less than one hundred years later, another Frenchman, Henri Giffard, figured that if he changed a few things, he could make the balloon idea work.

Giffard built an enormous, cigar-shaped balloon. But instead of hot air, he filled it with a gas called hydrogen. Hydrogen is lighter than air, so the balloon floated. A 350-pound (159 kg) steam engine turned a large propeller, which moved the airship through the sky. On his first flight, in 1852, Giffard puffed along at 6 miles (10 km) an hour and covered a distance of about 20 miles (32 km). In 1872 German inventor Paul Haenlein replaced Giffard's steam engine with an internal combustion engine, and the dirigible (steerable) balloon was born.

The Germans took quite a liking to dirigibles. They called them zeppelins, after Count von Zeppelin, who built several. By the 1910s, German zeppelins were carrying the world's first air passengers. During World War I (1914–1918), the German military tried using zeppelins in battle. But hydrogen is flammable, so zeppelins had a tendency to explode when hit by gunfire. They were also very slow compared to the smaller and more maneuverable airplanes being developed.

BARNSTORMERS

Before World War I, flying was just for a few aviation pioneers and adventurers. After the war, stunt pilots, called barnstormers, delighted crowds by wing-walking and spinning their planes in loop-the-loops.

Henri Giffard covers 20 miles (32 km) in a dirigible.
1852

The Wright brothers fly their first airplane at Kitty Hawk, North Carolina.
1903

A zeppelin airship in flight in the early 1900s

Airplanes and War

Airplanes changed the face of war dramatically. Before World War I, armies traveled on foot or by horse. But in an airplane, a fighter could fly deep into enemy territory, out of the range of guns on the ground. Armies began training fighter pilots and machine gunners to fly these dangerous missions.

The use of fighter planes fueled the aircraft industry. Many people found work in aircraft factories, building, servicing, and equipping the

The German military uses zeppelins during World War I.

1914–1918

WOMEN AVIATORS

In 1911 Harriet Quimby of Michigan became the first American woman to earn a pilot's license. Chicagoan Bessie Coleman became the first African American woman pilot in 1921. By 1937 Amelia Earhart was one of the world's most famous aviators. She had flown across the Atlantic Ocean twice and had completed a 2,400-mile (3,900 km) solo flight across the Pacific Ocean.

planes that rolled off the assembly lines in a steady stream.

When the war ended, Germany was the first country to use its old fighter planes to carry passengers. Britain, France, and the United States were quick to follow. By the 1920s, the commercial airline industry was already under way. But the peace didn't last very long, and by 1939, the world was again at war.

On December 7, 1941, the Japanese launched a surprise air attack on Pearl Harbor, a U.S. naval base on the Hawaiian island of Oahu. This bold act led the United States into World War II (1939–1945). Almost exactly four months later, the U.S. Army Air Corps answered the Japanese by attacking Tokyo, Japan, with a squadron (group) of sixteen B-25 bomber planes. Bombing targets from the skies proved a very effective way to fight. Airplane production in Europe, Japan, and the United States went into high gear.

When the war ended and the demand for bombers suddenly ceased, airplane manufacturers turned their attention to a peacetime public eager to get moving once again. The 1950s were a time of growth and prosperity in the United States. People had money

Japan uses planes to attack
Pearl Harbor, Hawaii.
1941

American Airlines begins
scheduled transcontinental
(U.S.) flights.
1959

to spend, and they wanted to travel. The war had brought about huge improvements in airplane design. The engines were more powerful. The seats were more comfortable. The aircraft were better equipped. Advertising on a new invention called television lured passengers aboard sleek silver planes that could take them just about anywhere they wanted to go. And they went. In droves.

We're Shri-i-i-i-nki-i-i-ing!

Thanks to the airplane, the world has become much smaller. At least it seems that way. Is this good or bad? Well, it's a little of both.

Airplanes carry us to faraway places in a very short amount of time. As long as there's a landing strip (and sometimes even if there isn't), we can fly to any spot on earth—and be there in less than twenty-four hours. Even Antarctica! Airplanes have opened up the world to vacationers, businesspeople, performers, athletes, and scientists. When the Napoleon Bonaparte of France headed off to Egypt in the late 1700s, the trip must have seemed endless. But modern travelers who want to see Egypt's wonders can hop on an airplane in the morning and be standing in front of the Great Pyramid at Giza before the sun sets.

Airplanes have also made it possible for doctors to reach patients in poor countries. Airplanes bring life saving medicines, equipment, and portable operating rooms to rural villages. The airplane helped to wipe out smallpox by transporting countless doses of the smallpox vaccine throughout the world.

The World Health
Organization begins a
campaign to end smallpox
worldwide.

1966

Epilogue

Not long ago, people dreamed of the twenty-first century as the amazing world of the future. Cars would fly. People would zip around in private rocket ships. Well, the twenty-first century is here. So what is really the latest in transportation inventions?

As for cars, they're still on the ground. But there are more of them than ever before. The convenience of having your own car appeals to many people. On the flip side, all these vehicles raise the level of air pollution. We are also using up our limited supply of petroleum, the natural resource used to make gasoline.

To help reduce pollution and dependence on petroleum, some automakers have developed hybrid cars. *Hybrid* means a cross between two things. Hybrid electric vehicles, for example, run partly on electricity and partly on gasoline. The Toyota Prius uses about 50 percent less gas than a conventional car its size and emits about 90 percent less pollution.

Big things are happening up in the sky too. In January 2005, the French company Airbus Industrie unveiled its superjumbo 380 airplane. From wingtip to wingtip, the Airbus A380 is 300 feet (90 m) wide—the length of a football field. It can seat as many as eight hundred passengers. It would take two or three average passenger jets to carry the number of travelers from one superjumbo. Fewer planes in the sky mean less air traffic.

The size of the superjumbo jet and the cost of a ticket may limit its use. An alternative would be a lighter, smaller passenger jet that could travel longer distances without refueling. Boeing, a U.S. company, is building its 7E7 Dreamliner out of plastic reinforced with carbon fiber (a strong, lightweight material). Because the 7E7 will be super light-weight, it will use 20 percent less fuel than other planes its size.

Newer technology in train travel may give both cars and planes a run for their money. Germany, Japan, and China are already using high-speed trains that run on electromagnets (magnets powered by electrical currents). Called maglev trains, they actually levitate, or float, on an electromagnetic current along guideways. Without the friction of metal wheels on metal tracks, maglev trains can reach speeds of 310 miles (500 km) an hour. They offer commuters and other travelers a convenient and speedy alternative to flying or driving.

Timeline

4000 B.C.	The horse is domesticated.
3500	The wheel is invented in Mesopotamia.
3000	The chariot and reed sail are invented.
600	The Phoenicians sail around the southern tip of Africa.
312	The Romans begin building the Via Appia.
A.D. 900s	The Vikings set out in ships to explore the North Atlantic Ocean.
1090	Chinese traders use a magnetic compass (a device that points to the magnetic North Pole) on a journey to the Middle East.
1270	Navigational charts, maps for sea travel, are used for the first time.
1347	The Black Death begins to spread across Europe.
1492	Columbus sets sail across the Atlantic Ocean, looking for a trade route between Europe and Asia.
1500s	Hungarians build the first four-wheeled coach.
1600s	Stagecoaches come into use in England.
1607	The London Company sends English settlers to North America.
1690	French scientist Denis Papin develops the first steam engine.
1765	After a British post office act, stagecoaches take over mail carrying in Great Britain.
1769	James Watt files a patent for a steam engine.
1783	The Montgolfier brothers launch a hot-air balloon from a Paris park.
1786	John Fitch builds and tests the first American steamboat.
1801	Richard Trevithick builds the first steam carriage.
1804	Trevithick builds the world's first steam locomotive.
1807	Robert Fulton's steamboat the *Clermont* travels from New York City to Albany, New York.
1814	Fulton begins a regular steamboat service on the lower Mississippi River.

1818 Karl Drais von Sauerbronn of Germany patents his bicycle.

1830 The Liverpool & Manchester Railway officially opens in Britain.

1838 The *Great Western* makes the first transatlantic steamship crossing in history.

1840s Waves of European immigrants begin arriving in the United States.

1848 The California gold rush is sparked by the discovery of gold at Sutter's Mill.

1851 The last clipper ship is built as sailing ships yield to steamships.

1866 The steamship the *Great Eastern* lays 2,700 miles (4,345 km) of underwater telegraph cable from Ireland to Canada.

1903 The Wright brothers' airplane takes flight in Kitty Hawk, North Carolina.

1908 The Ford Motor Company begins selling Model T automobiles.

1910s Dirigibles begin carrying passengers.

1913 Henry Ford begins using an assembly line at his Michigan auto factory.

1914 World War I begins.

1920s Airline companies begin offering commercial flights.

1941 Japanese planes attack Pearl Harbor, Hawaii, drawing the United States into World War II.

1947 Chuck Yeager passes the speed of sound in his Bell X-1 jet.

1959 American Airlines began scheduled transcontinental (between the U.S. East Coast and West Coast) flights of its Boeing 707 airplane.

1998 Toyota begins mass-producing the Prius, its first hybrid model.

2005 The French company Airbus Industrie unveiled its first super-jumbo passenger jet, the Airbus A380.

chariot: a two-wheeled cart pulled by a horse

commercial airline: a company that owns and operates its own airplanes and sells customers tickets on scheduled flights

Conestoga wagon: a covered, horse-drawn wagon used to carry people and goods to the U.S. western frontier in the 1800s

dugout: a small boat made by digging out the core of a tree truck

engine: a machine that converts energy into mechanical motion

fighter plane: a fast, maneuverable airplane equipped with weapons

internal combustion engine: an engine powered by mixing fuel with air and igniting it

locomotive: a railroad vehicle powered by an engine. A locomotive pulls (or sometimes pushes) the rest of the train along tracks.

navigate: to steer a ship or other vehicle from one place to another by determining its position and direction

stagecoach: a horse-drawn passenger or mail vehicle that runs on a regular route and makes stops at stations along the way

steamboat: a shallow boat powered by a steam-driven propeller or paddle wheel, used on lakes, rivers, and canals

steamship: a large, steam-powered ship usually used on larger bodies of water, such as the ocean

trade: the exchanging or selling of goods

transportation: a method of carrying goods or traveling from one place to another

SELECTED BIBLIOGRAPHY

Boorstin, Daniel J., et al. *Inventors and Discoverers: Changing Our World.* Washington, DC: National Geographic Society, 1988.

Cardwell, Donald. *The Norton History of Technology.* New York: W. W. Norton, 1995.

Carlisle, Rodney. *Inventions and Discoveries.* Hoboken, NJ: John Wiley & Sons, 2004.

Clark, Ronald W. *Works of Man.* New York: Viking, 1985.

Hodges, Henry. *Technology in the Ancient World.* New York: Knopf, 1970.

Hornsby, Jeremy. *The Story of Inventions.* New York: Crescent Books, 1977.

Knox, Noelle. "Longer, Taller Wider A380 Ready for Takeoff." *USATODAY.com,* 17 January 2005, http://news.yahoo.com/news?tmpl=story&u=/usatoday/20050117/bs_usatoday/longertallerwidera380readyfortakeoff (January 17, 2005).

Marcus, Alan, and Howard Segal. *Technology in America.* Orlando, FL: Harcourt Brace, 1999.

McNeil, Ian, ed. *An Encyclopaedia of the History of Technology.* London: Routledge, 1996.

Past Worlds: The Times Atlas of Archaeology. Maplewood, NJ: Hammond World Atlas Corp., 1988.

"Why the Future Is Hybrid." *The Economist,* December 4–10, 2004, 26–30.

Williams, Trevor. *A History of Invention.* New York: Checkmark Books, 2000.

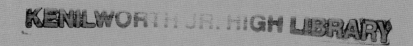

FURTHER READING AND WEBSITES

"Centennial of Flight." *U.S. Centennial of Flight Commission.*
   http://www.centennialofflight.gov
   This website commemorates the one hundredth anniversary of the Wright
   Brothers' 1903 flight. The kids' section features essays on French ballooning,
   wartime technology, commercial aviation, spaceflight, and daredevils and
   record-setters.

Coiley, John. *Train.* London: DK Publishing, Inc., 2000.
   Through many color and black-and-white photos, this books looks at the
   history, development, and impact of railroads.

Farman, John. *The Short and Bloody History of Highwaymen.* Minneapolis:
   Lerner Publications Company, 2003.
   Farman's book takes a fact-filled and humorous look at the highwaymen
   who plagued coach travel in seventeenth-century England.

Humble, Richard. *Submarines and Ships.* New York: Viking, 1997.
   Glossy overlays let readers see the insides of historical ships, including a
   Roman merchant vessel, a Chinese junk, an early submarine, and a luxury
   passenger ship.

Klaman, Bobbie, and Kate Calder. *Travel in the Early Days.* New York:
   Crabtree Publishing, 2001.
   This book explores travel in the United States before roads and bridges
   were common and looks at the changes brought about by steamboats,
   trains, and the early automobile.

Lavery, Brian. *Ship: The Epic Story of Maritime Adventure.* London: DK
   Publishing Inc., 2004.
   Lavery, a naval historian, explores how centuries of trade and exploration
   by ship have changed the world.

McPherson, Stephanie Sammartino, and Joseph Sammartino Gardner. *Wilbur &
   Orville Wright: Taking Flight.* Minneapolis: Lerner Publications Company, 2004.
   This well-researched and detailed biography tells the story of the Wright
   brothers and their quest for flight.

National Railroad Museum
http://www.nationalrrmuseum.org/
The National Railroad Museum website traces the history of railroading in the United States. "The Future of Railroading" looks at the continuing importance of this method of transportation.

Schlesinger, Arthur Meier, and Fred L. Israel. *Touring America Seventy-Five Years Ago: How the Automobile and the Railroad Changed the Nation.* New York: Chelsea House Publications, 1999. Originally published by the National Geographic Society, this books details the cultural impact of car and train travel in the United States.

"Transportation History." *Encyclopedia Smithsonian.*
http://www.si.edu/resource/faq/nmah/transportation.htm
This Smithsonian site provides links about air, sea, rail, and road transportation. There is also a link to the Smithsonian's own "America on the Move" exhibit, which looks at the impact of transportation advances on the United States.

Whitman, Sylvia. *Get Up and Go! The History of American Road Travel.*
Minneapolis: Lerner Publications Company, 1996.
Whitman looks at the innovations, inventions, and legislation that have shaped America's roads.

Woods, Michael, and Mary B. Woods. *Ancient Transportation.* Minneapolis: Lerner Publications Company, 2000.
This book charts the development of ancient travel technology, from vehicles to maps, lighthouses, bridges, and other innovations.

COVER AND CHAPTER OPENER PHOTO CAPTIONS

cover   Top: An ambulance wagon, flying the Red Cross flag, travels with a wagon train in the late 1800s. Bottom: A bullet train in Tokyo, Japan

pp. 4–5   Cars crowd New York City's Fifth Avenue in late 1913.

p. 6   King Cyrus of Persia enters Babylon on a horse-drawn chariot.

p. 16   Ancient Egyptian sailors relied on the wind in their papyrus sails to power their boats.

p. 22   A train runs under full steam in the late 1800s.

p. 31   A traffic jam in Philadelphia, Pennsylvania, in the 1950s

p. 40   Wilbur Wright looks on as his brother Orville makes the first powered aircraft flight in Kitty Hawk, North Carolina, on December 17, 1903.

pp. 46–47   The double-decker Airbus A380 superjumbo jet is the largest airliner ever built.

ABOUT THE AUTHOR Born in Baltimore, Maryland, Judith Herbst grew up in Queens, New York. A former English teacher, she ran away from school in her tenure year to become a writer. Her first book for kids was *Sky Above and Worlds Beyond*. Her other books include the Unexplained series, *Relativity*, and *The History of Weapons*.

PHOTO ACKNOWLEDGMENTS The images in this book are used with the permission of: Library of Congress, pp. 4–5 (LC-USZ62-107837), 11 (Lc-USZC4-3266), 13 (LC-USZC4-2634), 22 (LC-USZ62-70302), 24 (LC-USZC4-2758), 27 (LC-USZ62-56639), 32 (LC-USZ62-105442), 35 (LC-USZ62-111278), 40 (LC-W86-35), 43 (LC-DIG-ggbain-02131); © Bettmann/CORBIS, p. 6; © Kenneth Garrett, p.7; © Van der Heyden Collection/Independent Picture Service, p. 10; © Alinari/Art Resources, NY, p. 16; The Art Archive/British Museum/Harper Collins Publishers, p. 17; © H. Armstrong Roberts/CORBIS, p. 31; Ford Motor Company, p. 36; Courtesy of the Thomas B. Cavitt family, p. 39; © Handout/Reuters/CORBIS, pp. 46–47.
Cover photos: top, Library of Congress; bottom, © Chris Rainier/CORBIS.
Montgomery Ward & Co., back cover, p. 1, all borders